Times Before the Tales is the first step in the Times Tales® Series.

To the parents:

Before the student tackles mastery of the times tables, they must first understand the *concept* of multiplication and its connection with addition. Without this basic understanding, they may be able to compute multiplication problems (through memorization of the times tables) but will struggle with knowing *when to apply* this very important math skill. One effective strategy when introducing the *concept* of multiplication is to *visually* illustrate groups of objects.

Once the student understands multiplication as a language of groups, the next step is to illustrate the relationship of multiplication and addition when computing the facts. As the student progresses through this workbook, they should ask themselves the following two questions:

1. How many objects are in each group?
2. How many groups are there?

After having a basic understanding of the two elements (groups and number of groups) that come into play, the student realizes the answer can be computed using repeated addition (2+2+2+2...etc).

The Times Tales® 3 Part Series covers the 1's -12's multiplication tables.

©2022 Trigger Memory Co. 2nd Edition — Times Before the Tales

The First Step...Target the Lower Facts!

Times *Before* the Tales, introduces the multiplication tables focusing only on the lower facts (see chart below) which can easily be computed through skip counting and repeated addition, the process of adding equal groups together.

The Times Tales® 3 Part Multiplication Mastery Series breaks the 1-12 times tables down into three easy parts, utilizing three different methods to compute the facts. This chart illustrates how the multiplication facts have been divided into three segments.

#1 Times *Before* the Tales   **#2** Times Tales® (workbook or video)   **#3** Times *After* the Tales

Mastery Method: Skip counting and repeated addition.

Mastery Method: The Times Tales® mnemonic memorization method.

Mastery Method: The 11's & 12's times tables tricks.

Additional Reinforcement: Practice drills for lower facts.

Additional Reinforcement: Division related to multiplication.

Additional Reinforcement: Application of the time tables through 2-digit multiplication problems.

| CONCEPT | MEMORIZATION | APPLICATION |

Tackling the multiplication chart in 3 parts takes the stress out of learning the times tables.

For the sake of simplicity, we include the 5's & 10's tables in the "lower" times tables group, as these facts are most commonly computed through skip counting.

Times Before the Tales

©2022 Trigger Memory Co.

Conceptualizing Multiplication by Grouping

Times Before the Tales

Name: _____

Multiplication is having a certain number of groups, with the same number in each group.

 Since there are an equal number of balloons in each group, you can use multiplication to solve the total number of balloons.

❌ Since there are NOT an equal number of balloons in each group, you CANNOT use multiplication to solve the total number of balloons.

Can you use multiplication to solve the total number for these objects?

☐ Yes   ☐ No

Can you use multiplication to solve the total number for these objects?

☐ Yes   ☐ No

Can you use multiplication to solve the total number for these objects?

☐ Yes   ☐ No

First, draw your own groups with the same number of objects in each circle. Then, answer the questions below.

How many groups are there? _____   How many in each group? _____

©2022 Trigger Memory Co.

Times Before the Tales

Times Before the Tales

Name: _____

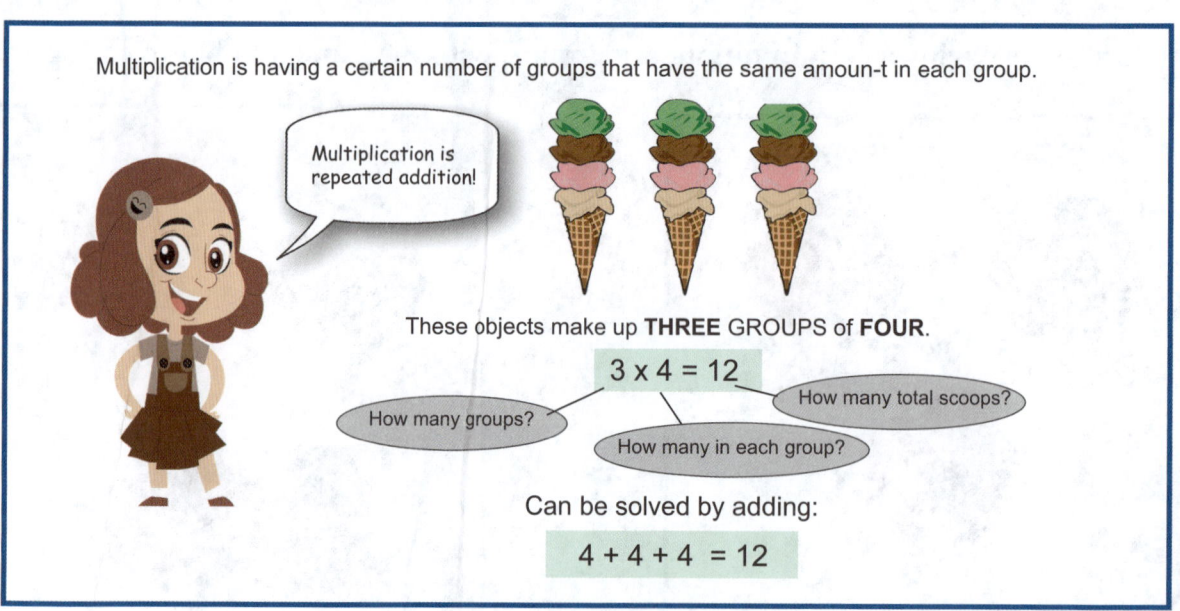

Fill in the circles with the correct number of dots based upon the multiplication problem. Then, solve using addition and multiplication.

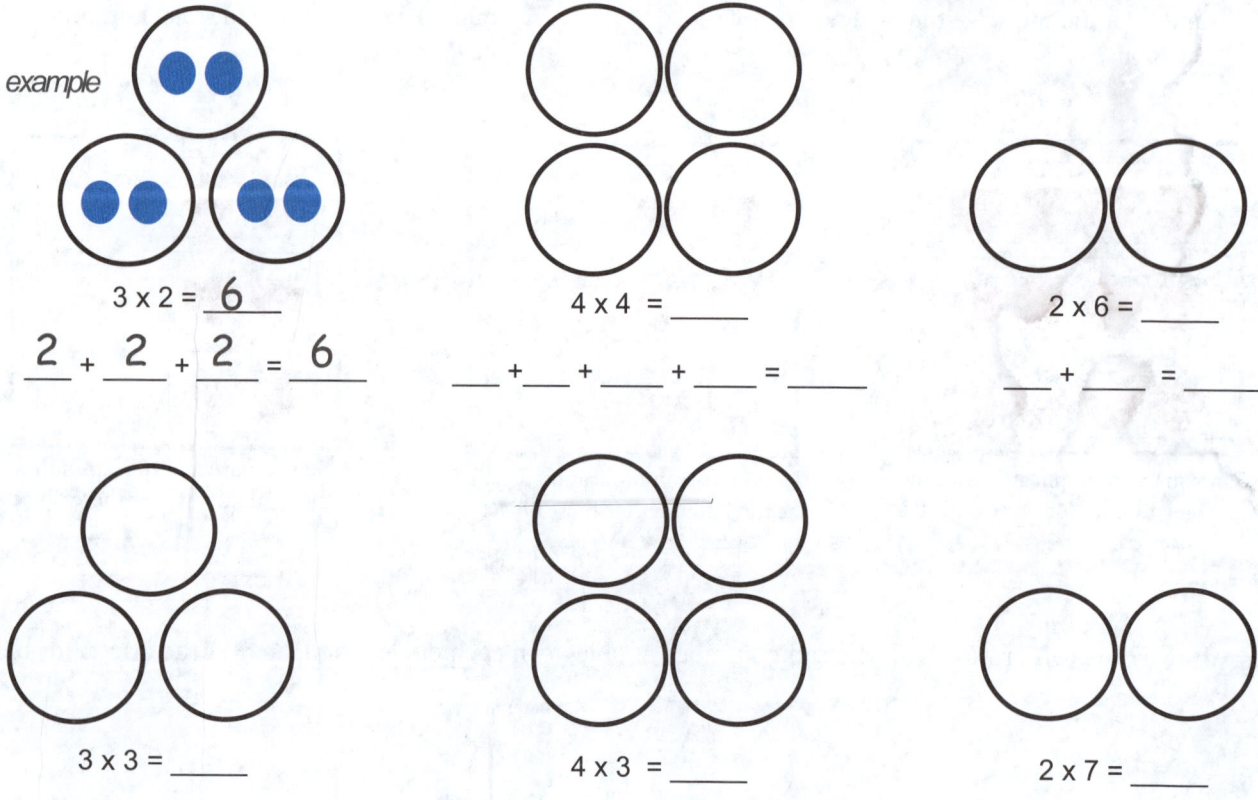

Times Before the Tales

Name: _____

(Continued from previous page).

1 x 1 = ____

____ = ____

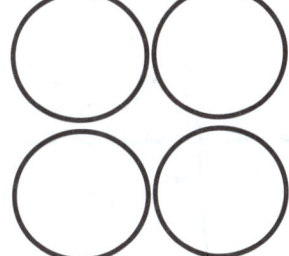

4 x 2 = ____

___+___+___+___ = ____

2 x 5 = ____

___+___ = ____

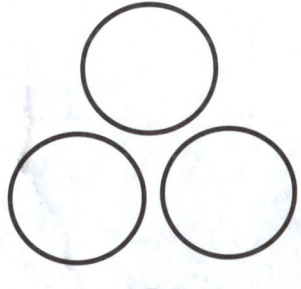

3 x 5 = ____

___+___+___ = ____

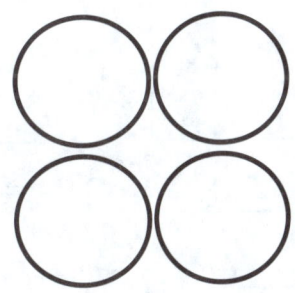

4 x 5 = ____

___+___+___+___ =

2 x 2 = ____

___+___ = ____

Draw ice-cream scoops on top of the empty cones based upon the multiplication fact. Then, use addition to find the answer.

___+___+___+___+___+___ = ____

6 x 2

©2022 Trigger Memory Co.

Times Before the Tales

Times Before the Tales

Name: _____

> 1. Cut out each multiplication problem at the bottom of the page.
> 2. Paste the math fact in the box with the correct grouping picture.
> 3. Fill in the answer to each problem on the line below each group.

| paste | paste | paste | paste |

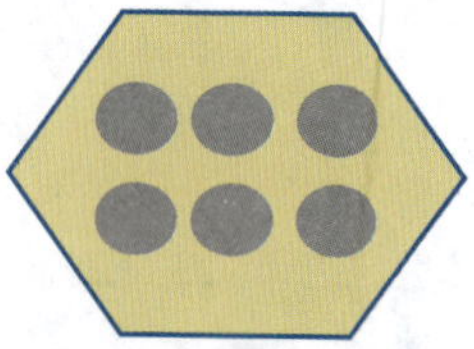

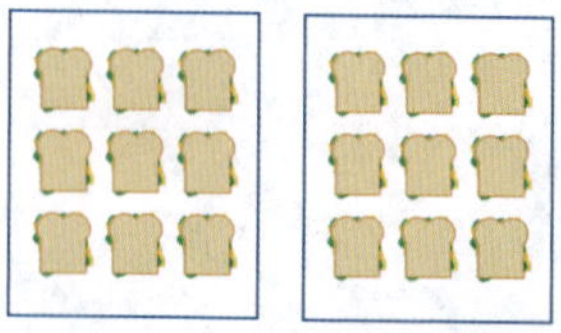

= _____   = _____   = _____   = _____

| paste | paste | paste | paste |

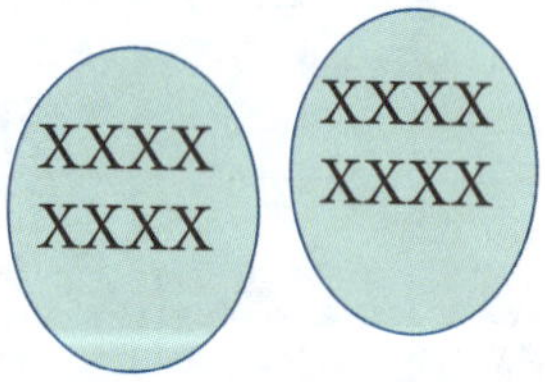

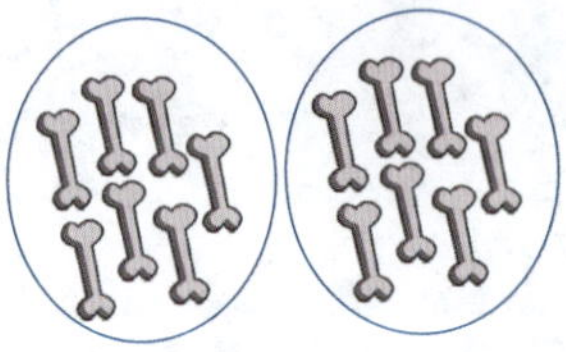

= _____   = _____   = _____   = _____

| 1 x 6 | 2 x 5 | 3 x 5 | 9 x 2 |

| 2 x 4 | 2 x 8 | 2 x 3 | 2 x 7 |

Times Before the Tales

©2022 Trigger Memory Co.

Times Before the Tales

Name: _____

Make your own multiplication facts by drawing an equal number of objects into each picture group. Then, write the multiplication problem in the box and the answer on the line below each group.

3 x 5 =

= 15 *example*

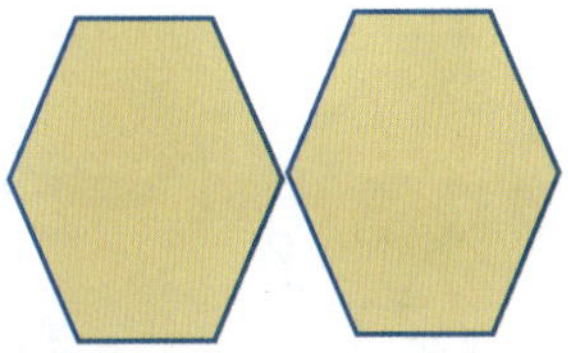

= _____

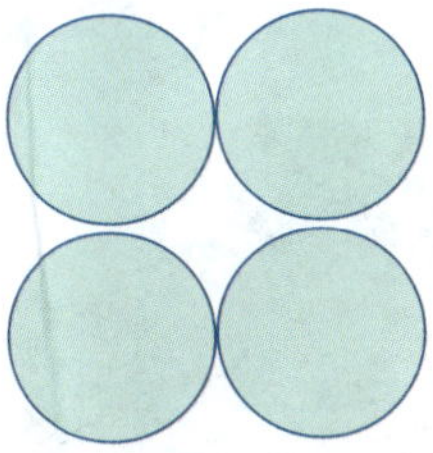

= _____

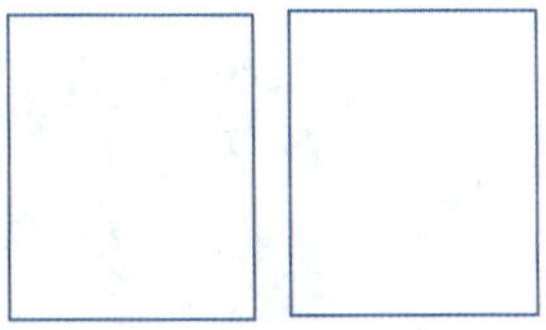

= _____

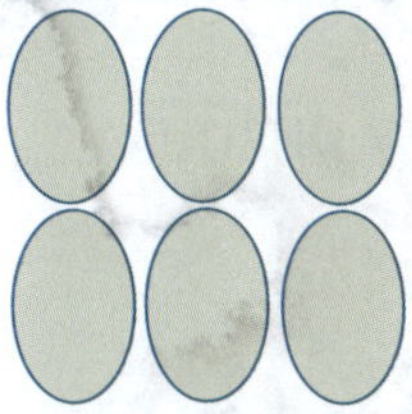

= _____

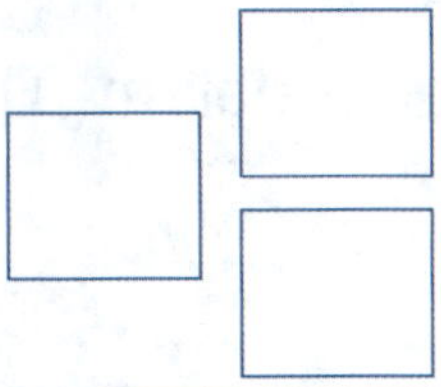

= _____

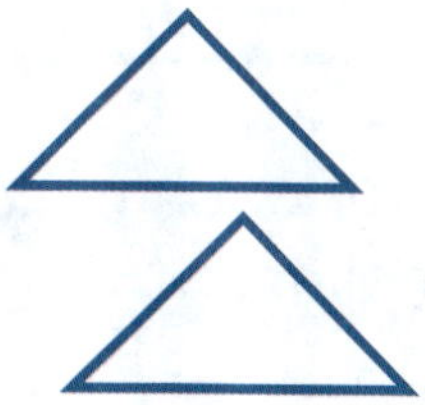

= _____

= _____

Fill in the multiplication and addition facts for each picture group below.

____ x ____ = _____

____ + ____ + ____ = _____

____ x ____ = _____

____ + ____ = _____

©2022 Trigger Memory Co.   Times Before the Tales

Times Before the Tales

Name: _____

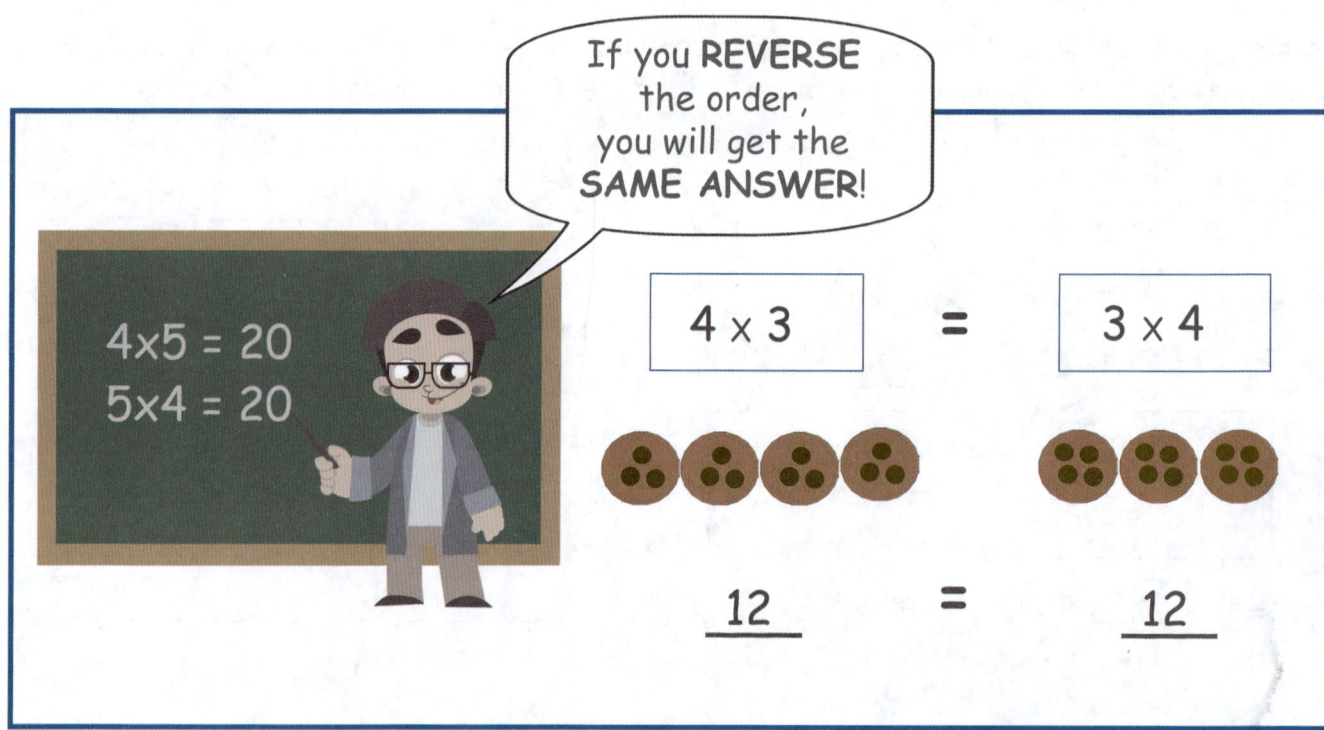

First, reverse the factors for each multiplication problem. Then, draw picture groups to show the examples.

4 × 3 = 12   example   3 × 4 = 12

5 × 3 = 15   ___ × ___ = 15

4 × 2 = 8   ___ × ___ = 8

Times Before the Tales   ©2022 Trigger Memory Co.

Times Before the Tales

(Continued from previous page).

Name: _____

10 × 3 = 30 ___ × ___ = 30

1 × 8 = 8 ___ × ___ = 8

4 × 5 = 20 ___ × ___ = 20

6 × 2 = 12 ___ × ___ = 12

2 × 3 = 6 ___ × ___ = 6

7 × 2 = 14 ___ × ___ = 14

©2022 Trigger Memory Co.

Times Before the Tales

Times Before the Tales

Name: _____

Find the total number of spots using multiplication.

![butterflies image]

_____ How many butterflies?

× _____ How many spots?

_____ How many spots altogether?

![cat image]

_____ How many cats?

× _____ How many spots?

_____ How many spots altogether?

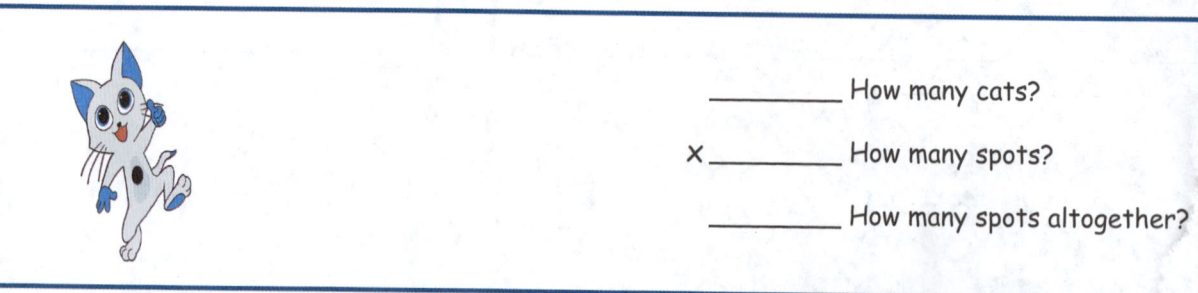

_____ How many ladybugs?

× _____ How many spots?

_____ How many spots altogether?

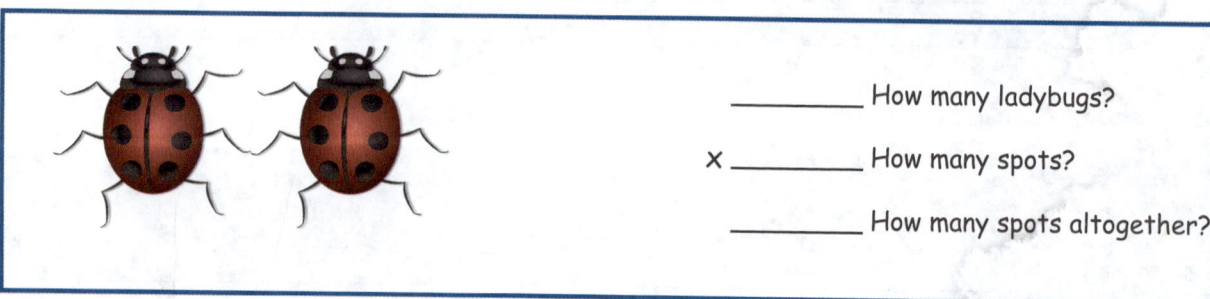

_____ How many turtles?

× _____ How many spots?

_____ How many spots altogether?

Times Before the Tales

Name: _____

I'd rather use multiplication than count each cookie one at a time!

Circle the groups of cookies for each multiplication fact. Then, write the answer.

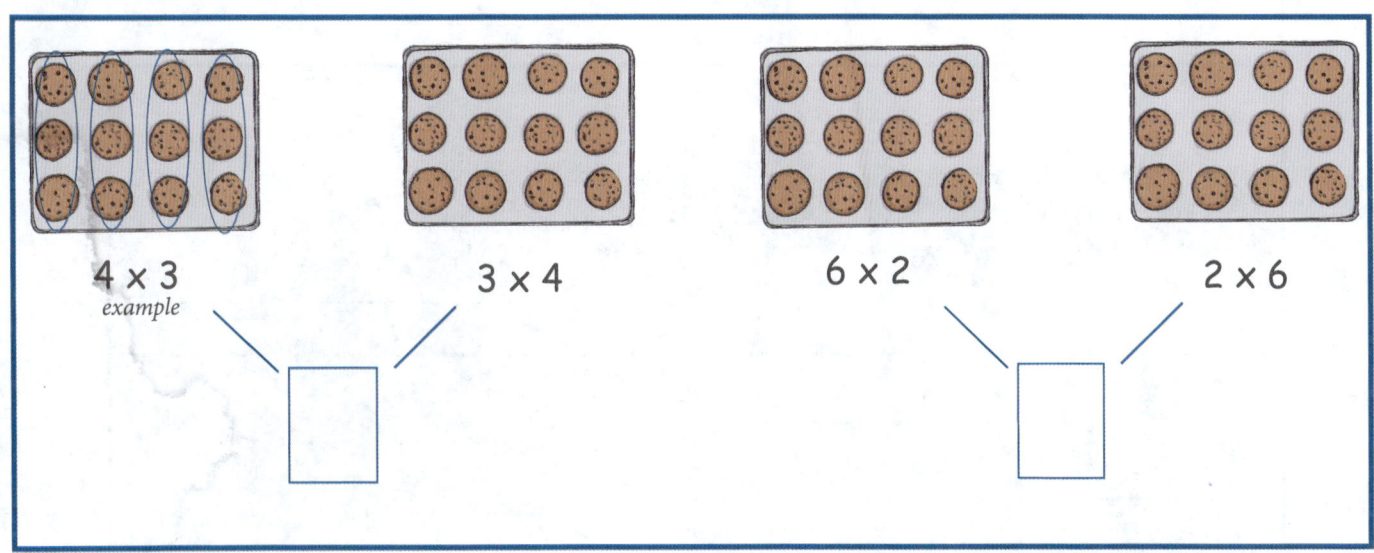

4 × 3
example

3 × 4

6 × 2

2 × 6

Draw the correct amount of chocolate chips on the empty cookies. Then write the total amount of chocolate chips.

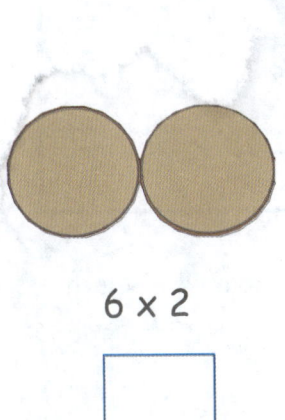

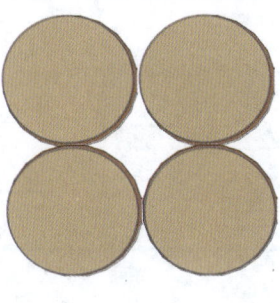

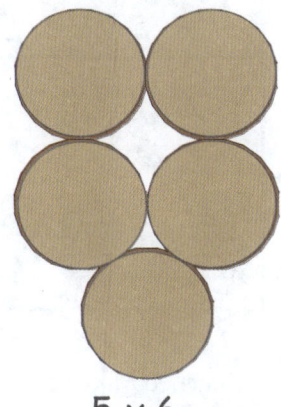

6 × 2

4 × 4

5 × 6

©2022 Trigger Memory Co.   Times Before the Tales

Times Before the Tales

Name: _____

Counting Money in Groups of Five

First, fill in each box with the number of $5.00 piles. Then, write the multiplication fact to solve the total amount of money for each group.

Groups of 5 ☐

How much altogether?

_____ x _____ = $___ ___.00

Groups of 5 ☐

How much altogether?

_____ x _____ = $___ ___.00

Groups of 5 ☐

How much altogether?

_____ x _____ = $___ ___.00

Groups of 5 ☐

How much altogether?

_____ x _____ = $___ ___.00

Joe earned $5 every time he walked his neighbor's dog. If Joe walked the dog 6 times, how much would he earn?

$5.00 x _____ how many times he walked the dog = $ ___ ___.00

Times Before the Tales ©2022 Trigger Memory Co.

Times Before the Tales

Name: _____

Connect the math facts with their correct picture groups. Then, solve the addition problem.

4 × 3		5 + 5 = __10__
8 × 2	 	10 + 10 + 10 = ____
4 × 4		9 = ____
9 × 1	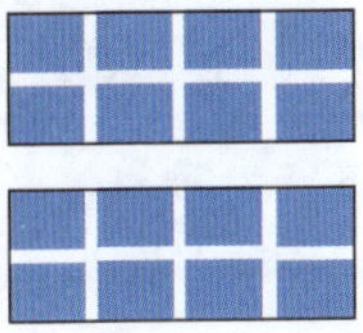 	4 + 4 = ____
10 × 3		3 + 3 + 3 + 3 = ____
5 × 2		8 + 8 = ____
4 × 2		4 + 4 + 4 + 4 = ____

©2022 Trigger Memory Co.

Times Before the Tales

Times Before the Tales

Name: _____

Write the addition and multiplication facts for each picture group below.

      There are 2 items in each bag. How many items are there all together?

_____ + _____ + _____ + _____ = _____

_____ × _____ = _____

   Ricardo read 3 books each month during his summer break. How many total books did he read for June, July and August?

_____ + _____ + _____ = _____

_____ × _____ = _____

   If Mia walks her dogs 5 blocks each day, how many blocks would she walk in 5 days?

_____ + _____ + _____ + _____ + _____ = _____

_____ × _____ = _____

   If one ride on the roller coaster cost 4 tickets, how many tickets would 4 rides cost?

_____ + _____ + _____ + _____ = _____

_____ × _____ = _____

Times Before the Tales   ©2022 Trigger Memory Co.

Times Before the Tales

(Continued from previous page).

Name: _____

 What is the total price for all the bags?

$_____ + $_____ + $_____ + $_____ + $_____ = $_____

$_____ × _____ = $_____

 If each student brought 10 cookies to a party, how many cookies would they have all together?

_____ + _____ + _____ + _____ + _____ + _____ = _____

_____ × _____ = _____

 If Daylen added $1.00 to his piggy bank each week, how much would he have saved in 8 weeks?

$____ + $_____ + $_____ + $_____ + $_____ + $_____+ $_____ + $_____ = $_____

$_____ × _____ = $_____

If each container has 9 pencils, how pencils are there all together?

_____ + _____ = _____

_____ × _____ = _____

©2022 Trigger Memory Co.

17

Multiplication Practice

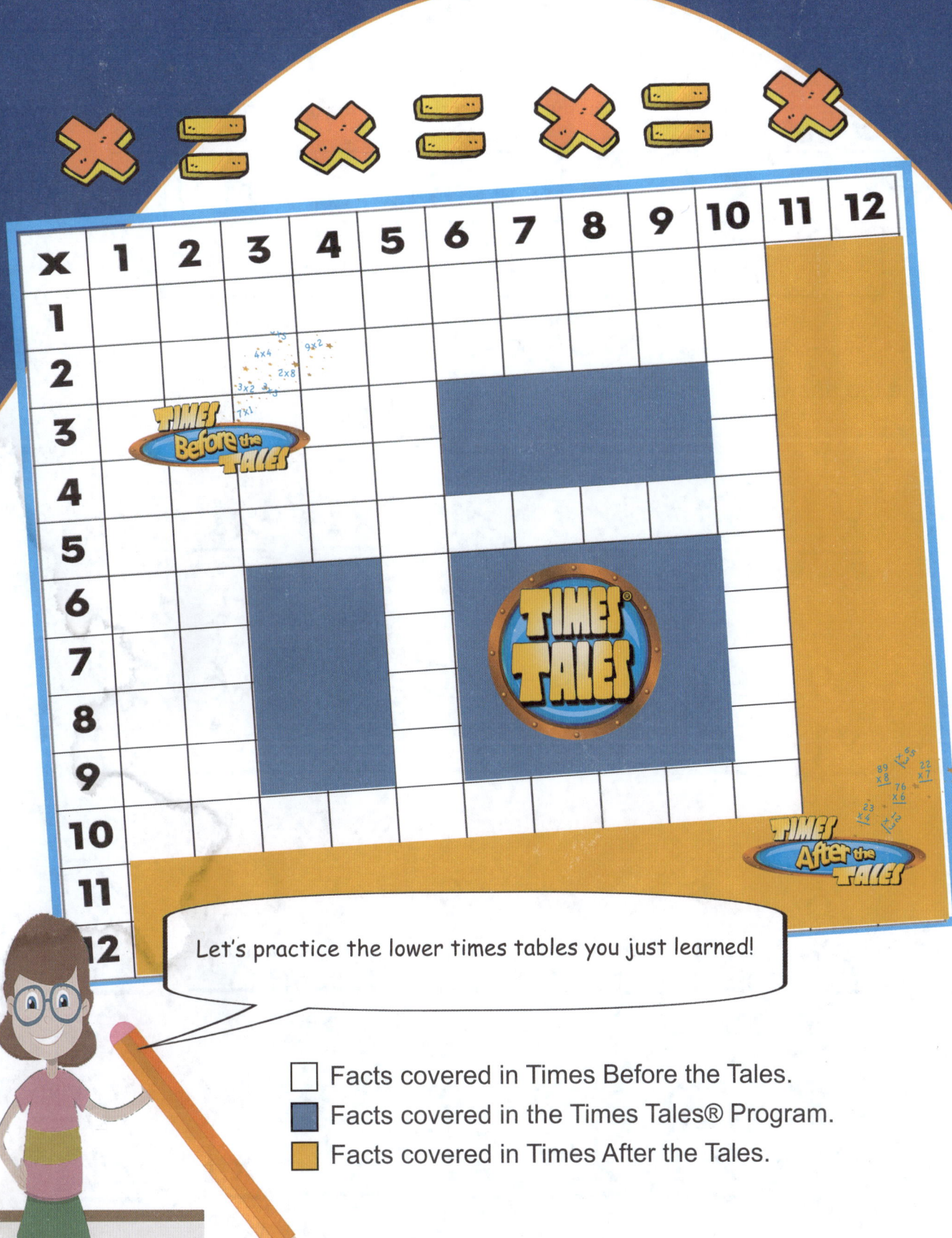

Let's practice the lower times tables you just learned!

☐ Facts covered in Times Before the Tales.
▨ Facts covered in the Times Tales® Program.
▨ Facts covered in Times After the Tales.

Times Before the Tales

Name: _____

Any number multiplied by 1 always equals the same number.

Fill in the multiplication chart boxes that are **not** shaded.

1s

X	1	2	3	4	5	6	7	8	9	10	11	12
1												

Times Tales® and Times *After* the Tales will cover the facts in the shaded boxes.

Write the answer to the multiplication facts.

```
  1       6      10       5       4       8       3
 x1      x1     x 1      x1      x1      x1      x1
 ___     ___    ___      ___     ___     ___     ___


  9       4       5      10       8       6       2
 x1      x1      x1     x 1      x1      x1      x1
 ___     ___     ___    ___      ___     ___     ___


  6       2       7       9       5       4       3
 x1      x1      x1      x1      x1      x1      x1
 ___     ___     ___     ___     ___     ___     ___


  8      10       5       9       3       4       6
 x1     x 1      x1      x1      x1      x1      x1
 ___    ___      ___     ___     ___     ___     ___
```

Times Before the Tales ©2022 Trigger Memory Co.

20

Times Before the Tales

Name: _____

10	8	9	5	10	9	3
x 3	x1	x5	x5	x 6	x10	x5

3	7	4	2	5	7	1
x5	x1	x4	x8	x2	x2	x5

10	4	8	10	10	8	6
x8	x2	x2	x 7	x 4	x5	x2

4	2	3	5	10	3	8
x3	x1	x3	x8	x9	x4	x1

2	4	7	5	9	10	5
x6	x4	x5	x3	x1	x 4	x8

2	10	4	10	1	6	3
x9	x6	x5	x10	x5	x5	x2

©2022 Trigger Memory Co.   Times Before the Tales

3 × 4 =	3 × 3 =	2 × 10 =
4 × 4 =	3 × 10 =	3 × 5 =
5 × 6 =	5 × 5 =	4 × 5 =

Cut Along Dotted Lines

5 × 9 =	5 × 8 =	5 × 7 =
10 × 7 =	10 × 6 =	5 × 10 =
10 × 10 =	10 × 9 =	10 × 8 =

Cut Along Dotted Lines

©2022 Trigger Memory Co.

Times Before the Tales